Baby Horses

 Bobbie Kalman

Crabtree Publishing Company

www.crabtreebooks.com

It's fun to learn about Baby Animals

Created by Bobbie Kalman

For beautiful Baby Gabrielle,
the newest little "Baude"
With much love from Bobbie, Peter, and Samantha

**Author and
Editor-in-Chief**
Bobbie Kalman

Editor
Robin Johnson

Photo research
Crystal Sikkens

Design
Katherine Kantor
Samantha Crabtree (cover)

Production coordinator
Katherine Kantor

Illustrations
Barbara Bedell: page 14
Katherine Kantor: pages 7, 24

Photographs
Marc Crabtree: pages 16 (bucket and hay),
     17 (bottom left and right)
© Dreamstime.com: page 7 (bottom)
© Shutterstock.com: cover, pages 1, 3, 4, 5, 6, 7 (top),
     8, 9, 10, 11 (all except middle), 12, 13, 14, 15,
     16 (top and bottom left), 17 (top left and right),
     18, 19, 20, 21, 22, 23, 24 (all except coats)
Other images by Digital Stock and Photodisc

Library and Archives Canada Cataloguing in Publication

Kalman, Bobbie, 1947-
     Baby horses / Bobbie Kalman.

(It's fun to learn about baby animals)
Includes index.
ISBN 978-0-7787-3953-1 (bound).--ISBN 978-0-7787-3972-2 (pbk.)

     1. Foals--Juvenile literature. I. Title. II. Series.

SF302.K33 2008   j636.1'07   C2008-900143-5

Library of Congress Cataloging-in-Publication Data

Kalman, Bobbie.
     Baby horses / Bobbie Kalman.
       p. cm. -- (It's fun to learn about baby animals)
     Includes index.
     ISBN-13: 978-0-7787-3972-2 (pbk. : alk. paper)
     ISBN-13: 978-0-7787-3953-1 (library binding : alk. paper)
     ISBN-10: 0-7787-3972-4 (pbk. : alk. paper)
     ISBN-10: 0-7787-3953-8 (library binding : alk. paper)
     1. Foals--Juvenile literature. 2. Horses--Juvenile literature. I. Title. II. Series.

SF302.K34 2008
636.1'07--dc22
                                                   2007052900

Crabtree Publishing Company

www.crabtreebooks.com   1-800-387-7650

Published in Canada
Crabtree Publishing
616 Welland Ave.
St. Catharines, Ontario
L2M 5V6

Published in the United States
Crabtree Publishing
PMB16A
350 Fifth Ave., Suite 3308
New York, NY 10118

Published in the United Kingdom
Crabtree Publishing
White Cross Mills
High Town, Lancaster
LA1 4XS

Published in Australia
Crabtree Publishing
386 Mt. Alexander Rd.
Ascot Vale (Melbourne)
VIC 3032

What is in this book?

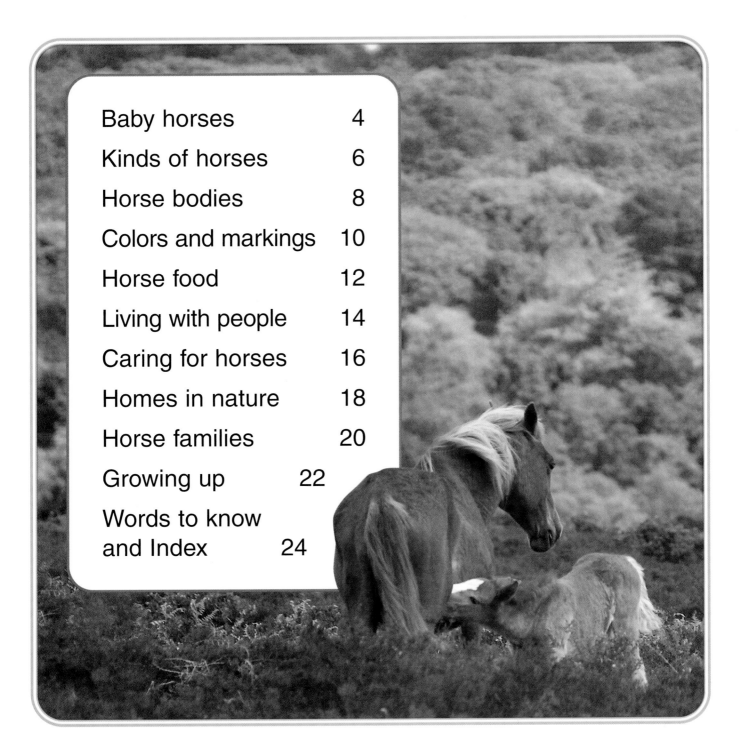

Baby horses

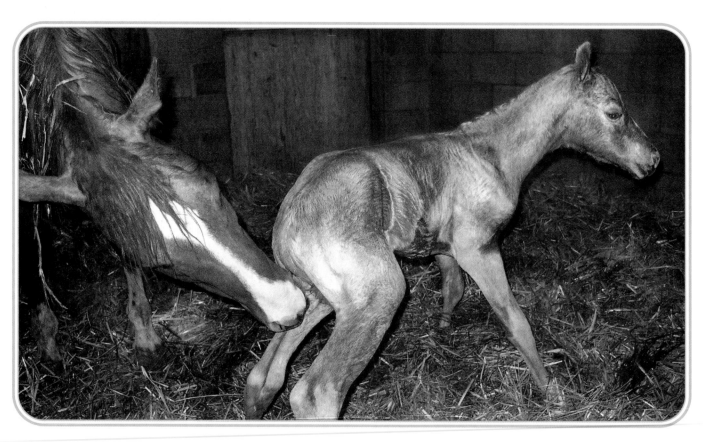

Horses are animals called **mammals**. You are a mammal, too. Mammals have hair or fur on their bodies. Horses have hair. Mammals are born. The baby horse on the left was just born. It will soon stand up.

*Baby horses are called **foals**. This mother horse is helping her foal stand up.*

Mammal mothers make milk inside their bodies. They feed their babies the milk. Drinking mother's milk is called **nursing**. Foals begin nursing soon after they are born.

This foal is nursing. Soon it will eat other foods, too.

Kinds of horses

Ponies are the smallest horses.

There are many kinds of horses. Some horses are bigger than others. Some horses live in nature. Most horses live with people. The horses below live with people.

This foal and its mother are Arabian horses. They are bigger than ponies.

Donkeys and zebras belong to the same family as horses. Donkeys are smaller than horses. They have big ears. Zebras have black-and-white stripes on their bodies.

This baby animal is a donkey. A donkey's ears are longer than a horse's ears are.

This baby and its mother are zebras.

Horse bodies

Horses have strong bodies. They have four long legs. Horses are **hoofed mammals**. Hoofed mammals have **hoofs** on their feet.

*The hair on a horse's neck is called a **mane**.*

A horse has a tail made of long hair.

*A horse has hoofs. Hoofs are hard coverings that protect a horse's feet. Hoofs are made of **horn**. Horn is a hard material.*

A horse has big eyes at the sides of its head. It can see almost all around its body.

hoofs

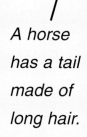

Horses have **backbones**. Backbones are the bones in the middle of an animal's back. Animals with backbones are called **vertebrates**. Horses are vertebrates.

*A vertebrate has many bones inside its body. All the bones make up the animal's **skeleton**.*

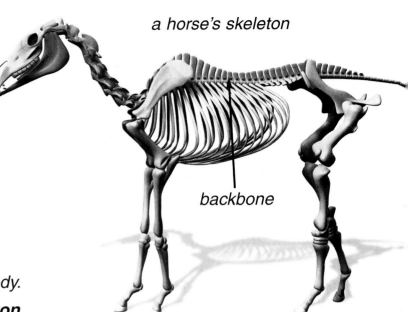
a horse's skeleton

backbone

Horse senses

Horses have strong **senses**. Senses are sight, hearing, smell, taste, and touch. Senses tell horses about the world around them. Horses smell and touch each other's noses when they meet. These foals are rubbing noses to say "hello."

Colors and markings

Horses have coats of short hair all over their bodies. They have longer hair on their manes and tails. The coats of horses can be white, brown, black, or **tan**. Tan is a light brown color. The horse on the left has a tan color.

*These horses are brown with white **markings**.*
Markings are marks made up of colors and shapes.

The coats of mothers and foals can be the same, or different. This mother horse is white with brown markings. Her foal is brown with white markings. Are their coats the same or different?

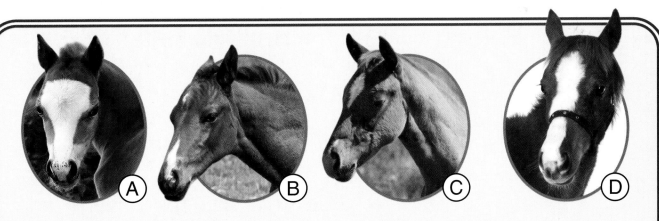

Some horses have markings on their faces, too. Guess which foal has each of these markings: a star, a snip, a stripe, and a blaze.

Answers: A has a blaze. B has a snip. C has a star. D has a stripe.

Horse food

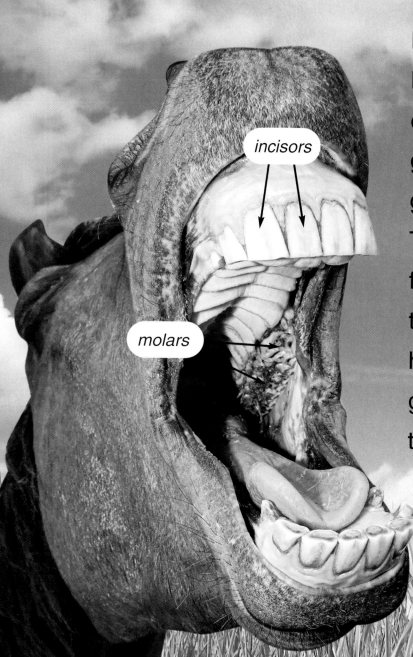

incisors

molars

Horses are **herbivores**. Herbivores are animals that eat mainly plants. Horses eat grass and other plants that grow close to the ground. They have sharp front teeth for cutting grass. Their front teeth are called **incisors**. A horse's back teeth are flat for grinding up food. The back teeth are called **molars**.

A foal drinks its mother's milk for up to a year. A few weeks after it is born, the foal starts eating plants, too. It also drinks water.

Living with people

*Horses live in barns called **stables**.*

Most horses live with people. A long time ago, people needed horses. Horses carried people from place to place. They pulled wagons and **sleighs**. Horses also did a lot of work on farms. Today, cars carry people, and machines do farm work. Most horses still live with people, however. People feed horses and care for them.

sleigh

*Some horses live on huge farms called **ranches**. Cowboys look after horses on ranches.*

People like to ride horses. This girl rides her pony every day.

Caring for horses

Horses that live with people need care. They need to be fed and **groomed**, or cleaned, every day. Most horses live and sleep in **stalls**. Stalls are living areas in stables. The stalls should be cleaned out every day.

This foal and its mother are in a stall.

water

hay

*Horses that live with people eat grass and hay. They drink water. This foal is **grazing**, or eating grass, in a field.*

This foal is getting exercise by running in a field. Its legs are getting stronger.

Riding is good exercise for both this pony and its young rider.

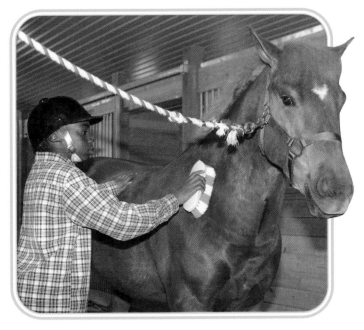

A horse's coat, mane, and tail must be brushed to stay clean.

A horse's hoofs need to be cleaned out every day.

Homes in nature

Some horses do not live with people. They live in the **wild**, or in nature. Horses that live in the wild look after themselves and their babies. They find their own food to eat.

*These Shetland ponies live in a **meadow**. A meadow is a grassy field.*

Horses in the wild live in different **habitats**. Habitats are the natural places where animals live. Some horses live in meadows. Some horses live on mountains. Some even live in very cold places.

This foal lives on a mountain.

Icelandic horses live in a place called Iceland. Iceland is freezing cold in winter.

Horse families

Horses live in big families called **herds**. Each herd has one **stallion**. A stallion is a male horse. A herd also has several mothers and their foals. The foals are protected by the herd. The herd keeps **predators** away from the foals. Predators are animals that hunt other animals.

Horses in a herd groom one another.

How many foals can you count in this herd?

How many horses are there in both herds?

Growing up

This mother horse has a baby inside her body.

A mother horse carries a baby horse inside her body. She carries the baby for about a year. Then the foal is born. The foal changes as it grows. The changes in the foal's life are called its **life cycle**.

A foal stands soon after it is born.

A few days later, the foal starts to run.

The foal joins its mother's herd. It stays close to its mother.

*When a foal is one year old, it is called a **yearling**.*

Between the ages of two and three, foals become adults. Adult horses can make babies of their own.

A new life cycle starts with each foal that is born.

Words to Know and Index

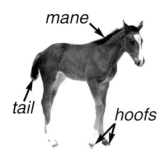

mane *tail* *hoofs*

bodies
pages 4, 5, 7,
8-9, 10, 22

markings

coats
pages 10-11,
17

donkeys
page 7

habitats
pages 18-19

herds
pages 20-21,
23

life cycle
pages 22-23

mothers
pages 4, 5, 6,
7, 11, 13, 16,
20, 22, 23

people
pages 6,
14-17, 18

ponies
pages 6, 15,
17, 18

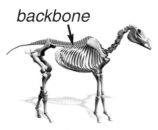

backbone

vertebrates
page 9

zebras
page 7

Printed in the U.S.A.